The Wreck of the "Rusty Nail"

Doonesbury books by G. B. Trudeau

Still a Few Bugs in the System
The President Is a Lot Smarter Than You Think
But This War Had Such Promise
Call Me When You Find America
Guilty, Guilty, Guilty!
"What Do We Have for the Witnesses, Johnnie?"
Dare To Be Great, Ms. Caucus
Wouldn't a Gremlin Have Been More Sensible?
"Speaking of Inalienable Rights, Amy. . ."
You're Never Too Old for Nuts and Berries
An Especially Tricky People
As the Kid Goes for Broke
Stalking the Perfect Tan
"Any Grooming Hints for Your Fans, Rollie?"
But the Pension Fund Was Just Sitting There
We're Not Out of the Woods Yet
A Tad Overweight, but Violet Eyes to Die For
And That's My Final Offer!
He's Never Heard of You, Either
In Search of Reagan's Brain
Ask for May, Settle for June
Unfortunately, She Was Also Wired for Sound
The Wreck of the "Rusty Nail"

In Large Format
The Doonesbury Chronicles
Doonesbury's Greatest Hits
The People's Doonesbury

a Doonesbury book by

GB Trudeau.

The Wreck of the "Rusty Nail"

An Owl Book **Holt, Rinehart and Winston / New York**

Published by Holt, Rinehart and Winston,
383 Madison Avenue, New York, New York 10017.

Published simultaneously in Canada by Holt, Rinehart and
Winston of Canada, Limited.

Library of Congress Catalog Card Number: 82-83139

ISBN: 0-03-061732-4

First Edition

Printed in the United States of America

The cartoons in this book have appeared in newspapers
in the United States and abroad under the auspices of
Universal Press Syndicate.

2 4 6 8 10 9 7 5 3 1

ISBN 0-03-061732-4

TODAY "TIME" MAGAZINE PUBLISHED ITS SIXTH LENGTHY EXCERPT FROM THE CONTINUING MEMOIRS OF HENRY KISSINGER. THIS YEAR'S INSTALLMENTS ARE FROM THE LATEST KISSINGER VOLUME, "YEARS OF WHITEWASH," ALSO PUBLISHED BY "TIME."

MEET HENRY GRUNWALD, EDITOR OF "TIME." MR. GRUNWALD, ISN'T YOUR MAGAZINE'S FASCINATION WITH KISSINGER BEGINNING TO TURN INTO AN OBSESSION?

NO, I THINK IT'S SOME-THING RATHER MORE SPECIAL.

MY EDITORS AND I HAVE BECOME THE KEEPERS OF THE KISSINGER FLAME. WE DOTE ON HIM, WE CONSULT HIM, WE WORSHIPFULLY TRACK HIS EVERY MOVE. HIS VIEW OF HISTORY, TO WHICH WE HOLD ALL THE RIGHTS, IS GOSPEL— UNEXAMINED AND IMMACULATE.

I SEE. SO IT'S MORE LIKE AN ORGANIZED RELIGION.

RIGHT. IN FACT, WE'RE APPLYING FOR TAX-EXEMPT STATUS.

WE'RE BACK AND RAPPING WITH DR. DAN ASHER, WHO HAS JUST SKYED IN FROM THE COAST TO HYPE HIS LATEST POP EPIC, "THE MELLOW PARENT: SHARING YOUR SPACE WITH DEPENDENTS."

LET'S TAKE IT FROM THE TOP, DOCTOR. WHAT'S YOUR ADVICE TO THE MELLOW MOTHER-TO-BE?

WELL, BASICALLY, IT'S TO GET IN TOUCH WITH YOUR BODY. MORNING SICKNESS, CRAMPS, ACHING BACK— JUST LET IT ALL HAPPEN!

ON THE BIG DAY ITSELF, GO ORGANIC. ANIMALS DON'T USE DRUGS, NEITHER SHOULD YOU. THE BIRTHING PROCESS IS BOTH VIOLENT AND BEAUTIFUL. GET INTO THE PAIN— EXPERIENCE IT FULLY!

AND YOUR ADVICE TO THE MELLOW HUBBY?

TAKE THE DAY OFF. SHOW SOME CLASS.

GBTrudeau

DR. DAN, IN YOUR PREFACE TO "THE MELLOW PARENT", YOU MAKE THE POINT THAT THE BIGGEST DECISION A COUPLE WILL EVER FACE IS **WHEN** TO BECOME PARENTS, RIGHT?

ASHBURYS

THAT'S RIGHT, MARK. TIMING IS THE HOT SUBJECT TODAY, ESPECIALLY TO WOMEN OVER 30. MANY OF THEM ARE TRYING TO BUILD CAREERS, BUT THEY HEAR THEIR BIOLOGICAL CLOCKS TICKING AWAY.

ASHTRAYS

THE MELLOW HUBBY SHOULD COMPENSATE BY BEING CIRCUMSPECT. EVEN IF HE INTENDS TO PARTICIPATE FULLY, HE SHOULD MAKE SURE HIS WIFE IS **UP** TO BOTH RAISING A KID AND BRINGING HOME THAT CRITICAL SECOND INCOME!

ASHBURYS

BUT HOW CAN HE TELL IN ADVANCE?

START HER OUT ON A PUPPY. SEE HOW MUCH IT EATS INTO HER TIME.

ASHBURYS

GB Trudeau

SENATORS, WHAT YOU'RE ABOUT TO SEE ISN'T PRETTY. BUT THEN, NAKED COMMUNIST AGGRESSION NEVER IS. MAY I HAVE THE FIRST SLIDE, PLEASE?

THIS, GENTLEMEN, IS A 57-mm SOVIET ANTI-TANK GUN. AS THIS U-2-GENERATED PHOTO SHOWS, IT IS BUT ONE ELEMENT OF A MASSIVE, CUBAN-ASSISTED ARMS BUILD-UP.

SOVIET ANTITANK GUN

SOVIET ANTITANK GUNS

EAST GERMAN TRUCKS

OTHER PHOTOS REVEAL RUNWAYS BEING LENGTHENED TO ACCOMMODATE MODERN JETS. FROM SUCH STRIPS, NICARAGUAN PILOTS CAN MOUNT SOVIET-BACKED ATTACKS.

TONY

NICK

ENGINES

HERE WE SEE A NICARAGUAN MiG-21 STRAFING A U.S. CRUISE SHIP..

HOLD IT, GENERAL.

GBTrudeau

..AND HERE, SENATORS, WE SEE A CONVOY OF SOVIET-MADE T-54 TANKS EN ROUTE FROM THEIR MANAGUAN DEPOT TO THE HONDURAN BORDER.

I HOPE YOU AGREE THE PHOTOGRAPHIC EVIDENCE WE HAVE SHOWN YOU THUS FAR IS BOTH IRREFUTABLE AND SHOCKING. UNFORTUNATELY, IT ONLY GETS WORSE!

RECENT U-2 FLIGHTS HAVE YIELDED NEW PHOTOS THAT CONCLUSIVELY DEMONSTRATE THE SERIOUSNESS OF THE COMMUNIST THREAT NOW FACING US! NEXT SLIDE!

HERE WE SEE A SOVIET GENERAL DIRECTING GROUND FIRE IN EL SALVADOR..

WHY DON'T WE TAKE A BREAK HERE, GENERAL?

GBTrudeau

GOOD MORNING, ALL, AND WELCOME TO THE WALDEN WAR GAMES. FOR THE NEXT HOUR, WE WILL BE RESPONDING TO COMPUTER SCENARIOS SIMULATING A NUCLEAR CONFRONTATION. THE PROGRAM IS MODELLED AFTER SIMILAR EXERCISES STAGED BY THE PENTAGON.

EACH OF YOU HAS BEEN ASSIGNED A PLACE IN THE CHAIN OF COMMAND. AS THE CRISIS GROWS, YOU MUST USE YOUR CODE BOOKS TO RELAY ORDERS TO YOUR STRATEGIC FORCES.

IN APPROXIMATELY 15 SECONDS, THE PROGRAM WILL APPEAR ON YOUR DISPLAYS. IF AT ANY TIME, YOU WISH TO TRY TO RESOLVE THE CRISIS THROUGH QUIET DIPLOMACY, SIMPLY PRESS THE CLEAR BUTTON.

READY?.. LET THE GAMES BEGIN!

CODE RED! CODE..UH.. NEVER MIND. JUST A FLOCK OF GEESE.

GBTrudeau

..AND WE'VE GOT ALL THE COMMIT-
TEE WORK DONE, AND IT'S GOING TO
BE A GOOD REPORT, SO I'M REAL
OPTIMISTIC, WHICH REMINDS ME, I
SHOULD CALL TREASURY, AND WILL
YOU LISTEN TO MS. MOTOR-MOUTH?

I'M SORRY, LACEY, I
DIDN'T MEAN TO RUN
ON AND ON LIKE THAT
AGAIN. I DON'T KNOW
WHAT'S THE MATTER
WITH ME LATELY.

I DON'T
EITHER, DEAR,
BUT IF I HAD
TO GUESS, I'D
SAY YOU'RE
PREGNANT.

WHAT?..
HOW DID
YOU..

MY GOD!
IT SHOWS
ALREADY?

IN A WAY.
SUSTAINED
EUPHORIA
ISN'T NOR-
MAL, DEAR.

GBTrudeau